CAUGHT SHORT

BRIAN HOWARD HEATON

89 WAYS TO PEE IN PUBLIC WITHOUT BEING SPOTTED

GRUB STREET · LONDON

Published by Grub Street,
The Basement, 10 Chivalry Road,
London SW11 1HT

A catalogue record of this book is
available from the British Library
ISBN 0-948817-60-7

Printed and bound in Great Britain
by Biddles Ltd, Guildford and
King's Lynn

BRIAN HEATON, who relieved one
set of frustrations in the heavily
researched classic *How to Have Sex
in Public Without Being Noticed*,
is now advising the reader on how
to cope with even more pressing
situations. He doesn't claim to have
been in everyone of them but has a
network of friends who are nothing
if not inventive.
Obviously a man of varying talents.
Light handcart available.
No Thursdays.

The Thinker

CHILDREN DON'T CARE THEY JUST LET RIP BUT GROWN UPS HAVE TO THINK MORE CAREFULLY...

AUCTION
THIS DAY

EASTERN
CERAMICS

THE
WHITE TOWER

NEWS STAND